THOUGHTS IN RHYME

KRITI BISHAKHA

Writing is my passion and this passion is only possible because of my mom and dad, I know its common to dedicate your work to your parents but its all because of them who supported me and made me that capable to write this and ofcourse my little sister because if I don't mention her this book is incomplete so here's this for you Chikky!

Also a special mention to the person who made me write so much about my unstable life!

Contents

Contents

Contents

Foreword

Being a reader of the poems I can definitely say it's really an interesting one! Well I am author's friend, writing is really a hard job even for the ones who has been doing it all the time and I really appreciate her dedication, she has also published many anthologies and I am sure this book will also touch your heart and help you to view the world with metaphors that Kriti has used.

I have been her friend since a long time and I have always seen her love and passion for writing, whenever she gets time she starts writing, yeah I am not the first one who reads it but not even the last, I always enjoy reading her poems and quote.

That's all I would say, do read this book and not keep it down till complete!

Happy Reading

Prologue

This book is all about poems which are based upon my life and mindset, so I am myself the main character of this book.

Acknowledgements

These are names of those people who are in some or the other way involved in publishing and writing of this book. Special thanks to Saheen Farhat for being Co-author of this book, it wouldn't have been possible without your contribution!

Tara Panda

Mrs. Chandrika Panda

Dr. Radhashyam Mishra

Khyati Mishra

Kiran Kumari Yadav

Subhasmita Mohanty

Preface

I have decided to write my unusual thoughts, about my unstable life ,my not so important advises which might be important for some and the lessons that I have learnt till now. These are all poems about my life and to be honest not everyone will relate to all of them. My work solely revolves around the commoyion hidden inside a young adult. Sure some of my initial poems mught seem immature but I still take pride in them since they are some of many reasons for which I am publishing this book.

This is my life, my story. It isn't perfect, but that's okay. I hope it helps many teenagers like me to feel good about themselves, learn to love yourself and adore yourself everytime!

Cheers!

Kriti Bishakha

@bishakha_346

1. LIKE NO OTHER

Like No Other

Like every brave soul do,
you may not succeed too
may be you not always win
but striving a bit is never a sin.
Like every shimmering star,
you may not always glimmer so far
everytime you have to suffer
but never slam your life's shutter.
Like every wonder hearts in peace,
you may not always inflate in ease
but trying again and again
will definetely give you something to gain.
But unlike other,
no matter what happens further
just smile and go on your way
this is what one has to say!

2. NO PROBLEM

No Problem

No problems is your life will stay forever,

They will pass away on day

So just shrug away all your anger,

Just try to be happy or happier.

Don't complaint even if you are

at unfortunate stage of your life,

Just shine like star and stronger you become,

Happiness is just here after this time,

Smile a bit everything's gonna be fine.

There's a lot problem in life,

your time will surely come soon,

Till then lear from it,

Adore it,

Understand it,

You will initially get out of it!

3. PAST DREAMS

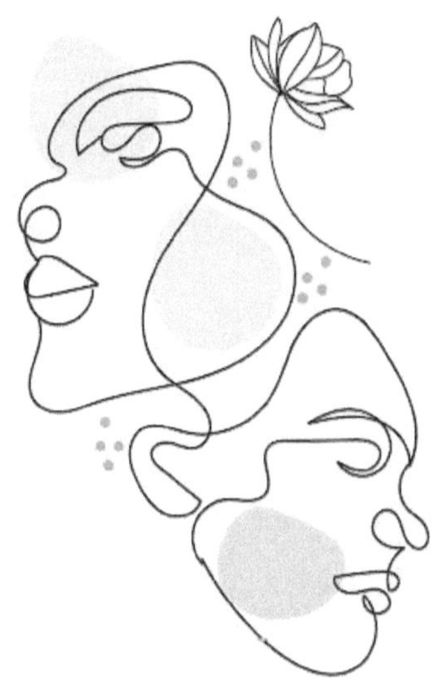

Past Dreams

The first day I say you,
everytime I felt I meant to you,
Never ever thought about future,
Being with you forever and ever,
Loved you, adorned you the most,
And one day everything lost.

A dark room became my life,
You came and filled it with ight,
Couldn't meet and see you always,
Deep inside my heart you were always present,
Happiness and love came from every side,
And one then one day,
Everything was lost.

Knocked the door of my heart,
And promised never to be apart,
Your presence was everything to me
your absence was too much hard to see,
You were my first and my last,
And one day
Everything became a past!

4. सपनों की मंजिल

सपनों की मंज़िल

मंज़िलों कि तलाश में,
कुछ सपने यूँ चल पड़े।।

सफ़र से अनजान बस,
अंधेरों में राह बनाने लगे।।

छोटे-छोटे पैरों से डगमगाने लग,
बड़े होते-होते रास्ते पर दौड़ने लगे।।

पंख जो मिले इन्हें,
आसमान को छूने उड़ने लगे।।

सितारों कि मेहफ़िल में,
अपनी रात सजाने लगे।।

सूरज की धूप जो चुभने लगी,
तो थककर पेड़ की छांव में सोने लगे।।

वक्त कब आगे बढ़ गया पता ना चला,
कुछ टूट गए, कुछ ठहर गए, कुछ अब भी चल रहे।।

चलते चलते न जाने कहाँ खो गए, अपनी ही सांसों से दूर होने लगे।।

फिर भी रूका नहीं सपनों का कारवां,
क्योंकि चमक रहा था ये अभी भी सितारा बनके।।

5. मेरे साथी मेरे हमराही

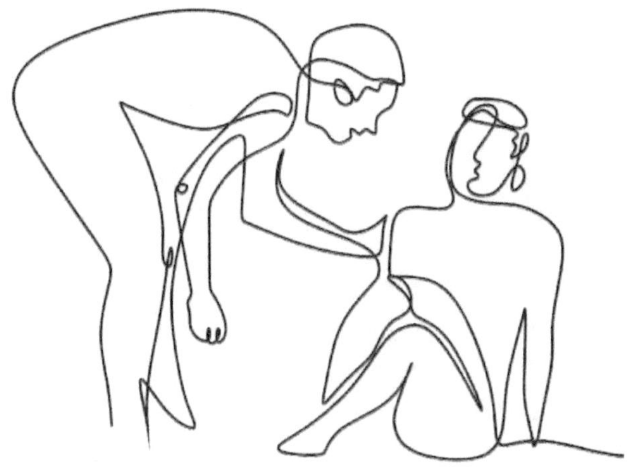

मेरे साथी मेरे हमराही

मेरे साथी मेरे हमराही
तू उदास न हो,
माना ये समय कठीन है
मगर तू हिम्मत न छोड़।
आंखों में आशा की
किरण लिए तू चल,
बिखरे जो रिश्ते
उन्हें संभालते हुए चल।
कदम कदम पे मुश्किलें
चट्टानों सी खड़ी हैं,
मगर तू उन्हें तोड़कर
पार कर निकल।
मेरे साथी मेरे हमराही
तू हिम्मत न छोड़,
माना ये समय कठीन है
मगर तू हिम्मत न छोड़।
अपने सपनों को याद कर
उनकी तलाश में चल,
मंजिल कठीन है
पर असंभव नहीं,
जो तेरा साथ दें
उन्हें अपनी हिम्मत बनाते चल,
कमज़ोरी को भूल
अपनी मंज़िल की ओर चल।
मेरे साथी मेरे हमराही
तू उदास न हो,
माना ये समय कठीन है
मगर तू हिम्मत न छोड़।।

6. कुछ पल

कुछ पल

ज़िंदगी का एक और वर्ष कम हो चला,
कुछ पुरानी यादें पीछे छोड़ चला।
कुछ खुशियां दिल में रह जाती हैं,
कुछ बिन मांगे खुद ही मिल जाती हैं।
कुछ छोड़ कर चले गए,
कुछ नए इस सफर में जुड़ गए।
कुछ मुझसे दूर हो खफा हो गए,
कुछ मुझसे पास हो खुश हो गए।
कुछ अब भी यादों में बसें हैं,
कुछ पास होके भी भूल गए हैं।
कुछ शायद अनजान हैं,
कुछ बहुत परेशान हैं।
कुछ को मेरा इंतजार है,
कुछ का मुझे इंतज़ार।
कुछ सही है,
कुछ गलत भी।
कुछ हो सके तो हमें माफ कीजिए,
कुछ अच्छा लगे तो जरूर याद कीजिए।।

7. नए ख़्वाब

नए ख्वाब

देखकर नए कुछ ख्वाब खुद को जगाया करो,

रातें तुम अपनी अक्सर किताबों की शब्दों में बिताया करो।

मंजिल आएंगी हाथ तुम्हारे किसी समय तो,

तुम आंखों में अपने सपने सजाया करो।

आकाश को देख तुम उन उचाइनयों तक उड़ो

पंख जो टूटें उन्हें संभाल फिर उड़ चलो।

कहने दो लोगों को उनका तो काम है कहना,

तुम खामोशी को अपनी तलवार बनाए चलो।

हार जाएगी उदासी तुम्हें यों देखकर

बेवजह भी कभी तुम मुस्कुराया करो।

खुद रो खुद की बातें कहो।

थोड़ा समय एकांत में भी बिताया करो।

उठा सकोगे लुफ्त ज़िंदगी का

बस खुदको सबसे अलग बनाते रहो।

रुलाए कभी जो तुम्हें ये ज़िंदगी तो,

मां के आंचल में वक्त बिताया करो।।

8. ज़िंदगी एक किताब

ज़िंदगी एक किताब

ज़िंदगी काश तू एक किताब होती,

पढ़कर सारे पन्नों को

जान पाती की आगे तू कैसी होती

क्या ये मेरा दिल पाएगा

और कौन मुझसे दूर जाएगा

कब खुशियां आयेंगी और

कब ये सारा गम जाएगा।

ज़िंदगी काश तू सचमुच एक किताब होती,

फाड़कर सारे उन लम्हों को

जिन्होंने मुझे रुलाकर तोड़ा है

जोड़ देती कुछ ऐसे पन्ने

जिन्होंने मुझे हंसाया है

हिसाब तो लगा ही पाती

कितना खोया और कितना पाया है।

काश ज़िंदगी तू सचमुच एक किताब बन जाती।।

9. IF YOU ASK

If You Ask

If you are asking,

If I need you,

My answer will be

Yes I do.

If you are asking,

If I'll ever leave you

My answer will be never ever.

If you are asking,

What's most valuable to be

My answer will be

YOU.

If you are asking,

Do I love you

My answer will be

Yes I do, I do

Very much I do!

10. A GIRL OF HER HEART

A Girl of Her Heart

A girl inside me,
is somewhere living in dark,
finding some missing puzzles,
but again and again falling apart.

Silence and silence everywhere,
Anwers of her questions
Are still unaware,
Her heart is in search of
that one little voice
yet she is surrounded
By noises and noise.

There's war between her heart and brain,
Very dissapointed she is
with laboured ease of pain,
She us waiting and waiting
for that one fine day,
Till then she us just
Silent, silent and silent everyday.

11. GUARDIAN OF TOMORROW

Guardian of Tomorrow

What this world has become,

Humans are dying,

Animals are crying

Trees are cut without any meray

Rivers are drying without any rain.

Oh! What this world is,

But there's someone

Who can save us all

It's the one within us

Brave, confident, determined and strong.

We little humans,

Are tomorrow's bright future

Our little help of today

Can make us great the next day.

So let's all of us get together

Don't let now any glacier to melt,

Don't let now any trees to cut

Even if it's done

Then let's promise to be

The Guardian of Tomorrow!

12. ONE QUESTION

• 47 •

One Question

Where's my path going?
yet unknown is my soul what's my heart saying?
Is so confusing for my mind alone and desperate
that's what you have made me.
Where is my life going?
yet unknown is my soul
What's going to happen tomorrow?
will anyone please tell me?
Anxious fellow why don't you die now?
When will it over I am tired now.
All over my mind,
Only a question revolves
Over thinker me,
Will you ever stop somehow?

13. ये बता नहीं सकती

ये बता नहीं सकती

ये बता नहीं सकती

क्या सोचती हूं यह बता नहीं सकती,

हाल अपने इस दिल का जता नहीं सकती,

तेरी यह मुस्कुराहट जैसे ख्वाब सा है,

बारिश की बूंदों के एहसास सा है,

काश तुझे यह मैं बता सकती।

तू ही हर पल मेरे ख्वाबों में,

क्या करूं तुझे सोचे बिना रहा नहीं जाता,

खो जाने का दिल जाता है तेरी बातों में,

काश कि हर लम्हा हर घड़ी,

हर पल तू ही मेरे पास होता।

पर काश की मैं यह सब कह सकती,

अपने दर्द ए दिल का हाल बता सकती,

पर एक ही डर सताए हर पल,

तुम मुझसे दूर हो जाए,

इसलिए तुझे कुछ बता नहीं सकती।।

14. मैं रो नहीं सकती

मैं रो नहीं सकती

मेरी आंखों में आंसू हैं,

मगर मैं रो नहीं सकती

सफलता के पंख कट गए

तो क्या मैं फिर उड़ नहीं सकती?

लोग ताने मारते रहे,

मेरी दुर्दशा पर हस्ते रहे

तानों को इस भारी बोझ को

अब मैं उठा नहीं सकती,

मेरी आंखों में आंसू हैं

मगर मैं रो नहीं सकती।

गम के बादल छाए हुए हैं,

मुश्किलों के तूफान आ रहे हैं

लेकिन एक रात के बाद सुबह न आए,

ऐसा हो नहीं सकता,

मेरी आंखों में आंसू हैं

मगर मैं रो नहीं सकती।

हारी बाज़ी को मैं एक दिन,

ज़रूर जीत कर दिखाऊंगी,

बिना अपने मंजिल को पाए,

अब मैं सो नहीं सकती।

15. चल पड़ तू

चल पड़, तू

किन ख़यालों में खोया है तू?

आसमान के उन तारों को छोड़

कहां ज़मीन पर पड़े कंकड़ गिन रहा है तू।

किस उड़ान की चिंता में बैठा है तू,

जिसकी कोई उड़ान की गति ही न हो,

उस ऊंचाई को क्या छू पाएगा तू?

देख आंख खोल सामने पहाड़ तू,

पार करने की इच्छा लिए,

चल पड़|आज सारे मोह त्याग तू।

16. मां

मां

उसकी एक आवाज़ से

सारी खुशियां मुझ में समा जाए,

मां तेरे बिना सब कुछ

सूना सूना सा बन जाए।

तेरी गोदी पे सिर रख

सारी रात तेरी लोरी सुनूं,

तेरी नम आंखों भरी मुस्कान से

पूरी दुनिया जीत लूं।

तू जो नाराज़ हो जाए,

तो मेरी ये सांस थम जाए,

तुझ बिन एक पल भी,

सौ जनम जैसा बन जाए।

तेरी याद, तेरा साथ,

सबके बिना मैं अकेली हूं मां,

एक बार मेरे पास आजा,

एक बार मुझे गले लगा जा।

तेरी प्यार की कमी,

बहुत सताती है मां,

तेरी गोदी, तेरा प्यार

मुझे हर पल याद आए

मुझे हर पल याद आए मां।।

17. इश्क़

इश्क़

क्या है ये इश्क मेरा?

मुश्किलों में ये डाले

जो दिल चाहे वो करा ले,

न सोचे ये आगे की,

न आए ये पीछे कभी,

रोका जाए ना रोक से,

कैसा है ये इश्क मेरा?

रिस्क कहो या चाहत,

किन राहों पर ले चले

उसकी होती भी नहीं कोई आहट,

बिन दस्तक दिए

खुद ही पहुंच जाए

दर्द कहो या खुशी

ये तो बस अब इसकी मर्जी

इतनी उलझन है मेरी

कोई तो सुलझाए?

18. तू न आया

तू न आया

तेरी यादों में,

मेरी नींदें गुम गईं,

कितनी बातें थाम गईं

पर तू न आया।

रातें मेरी नाम आंखों से भरी,

चाहतें मेरी अब टूट सी गईं,

इतनी बार हो गईं,

पर तू न आया।

जीना तो बस,

अब सांस लेना ही रहा,

जो कभी मेरा था

न जाने किस ओर चला

वक्त तो आगे बढ़ता गया

पर तू न आया।।

19. इंतजार

इंतजार

तेरी बांतों की इंतज़ार में,

मेरी सारी दिन बीत जाती,

तू आएगा ये सोच

मैं खुद को दिलासा देती।

तेरे मेरे बीच की ये हो दूरी है,

कैसे जानू की क्या तेरी मजबूरी है

चाह के भी एक पल देख न पाऊं,

तेरी एक झलक में सारी खुशी पा जाऊं

तुझ बिन एक दिन एक जनम सा लगे,

मेरी आसुओं को आज तुम समझ न सके।

ये कैसी अजीब सी बैचैनी है,

मुझसे दूर हो जाने की ऐसी क्या तेरी मजबूरी है?

20. तेरा साथ न मिला

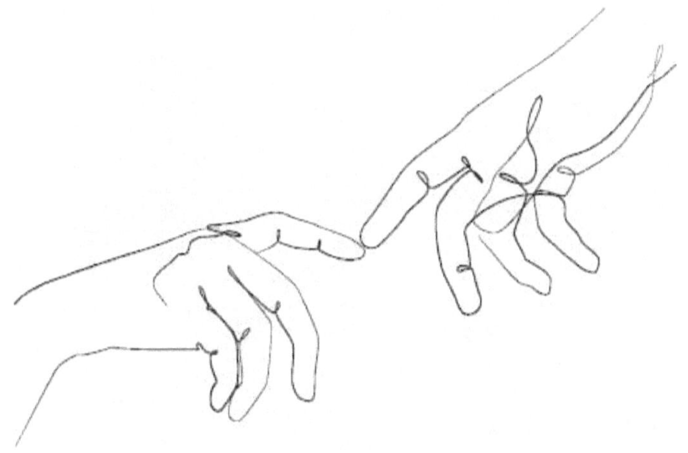

तेरा साथ न मिला

हाथ थाम कर भी सहारा न मिला,

मैं त्रो लहर हूं जिसे किनारा न मिला।

मिल गईं त्रो सारी चीज़ें जो भी चाहा मैंने,

मिला नहीं तो सिर्फ साथ तेरा न मिला।

वैसे तो सितारों से भरा हुआ है आसमान,

मगर जो मैं ढूंढ रहा था त्रो सितारा न मिला।

कुछ इस तरह से बदली ज़िंदगी ये मेरी,

फिर जिसको भी पुकारा त्रो दुबारा न मिला।

एहसास तो हुआ उसे मगर देर हुए बहुत,

उसने जब ढूंढा तो निशान भी न मेरा मिला।।

21. A CUP OF COFFEE

A Cup of Coffee

A Cup of coffee,
A latte or a mocha
An espresso or cappuccino
Either of them will do.

When you take a sip,
and it touches the lip
Gives you that happiness,
that you can't even think.

A cup of coffee,
Espresso or flat white
you may not add any sugar
The taste is always right.

This coffee is the one,
who really loves me a lot
Brings a lot of happiness,
in it's bittery beans.

22. WINTER MEMORIES

Winter Memories

When the days are shorter
and nights are long,
The moon is cruel,
And the wind is like a sword.
Cold memories flashed upon,
When you and me
were sliding down frozen hills,
And ran between the snowy mills.
On those chilly snowy days,
When we were the happiest,
never ever felt alone,
and time was passing on and on.
No matter how cold,
the outside world was,
The blanket of your love,
Gave me all the the warmth.
Today, my heart cries,
missing the one whom it loves,
nights have become longer and longer,
But our snowy memories,
Don't end here!

23. AROMA OF COFFEE

Aroma of Coffee

That sweet aroma of coffee
fills the little room of my heart,
Brewed and tackled many issues,
Created many solutions,
Without being harsh.

That sweet aroma of coffee
Lits many romantic candles,
Brings out the sweet words within you,
Love and feelings were expressed so far.

That sweet aroma of coffee
made enemies even friends,
Hurt and hatred could mend,
Various cold and small wars could end.

Isn't this aroma wondering?
Which made anything possible,
without any sort of violence
Good things came out
just with that aroma of coffee.

24. इस बार

7

इस बार

आंखों में आंसू है,

पर चेहरे पर मुस्कान,

मेरी दिल की बैचैनी को तू,

समझ न सका इस बार।

तेरे मेरे बीच की ये दीवार,

तोड़ती जाती मुझे बार बार,

मेरी मन की उदासी को तू,

समझ न सका इस बार।

आखिर क्या ऐसी मजबूरी है,

तेरे मेरे बीच की ये जो दूरी है,

मेरी ख्वाहिशों को टूटता देख तू,

समझ न सका इस बार।

हार दिन हर घड़ी,

बस तेरी जी इंतज़ार में रही,

मेरी बेबसी को क्यों तू,

समझ न सका इस बार?

25. MY VISION FOR INDIA

My Vision for India

Making our country,
from developing to developed,
Having a great mission,
Is the vission of our nation.

Making our country,
free from hunger and fear,
Happiness brightening every faces,
No eyes are in tears.

Making our country,
A Powerful example for all,
No differences in colour or creed,
Equally celebrating ever festive!

Making our country,
A highly literate state,
I to **Me** and **My** to **Our**
Is my vision for our nation

26. PEACE ON EARTH

Peace on Earth

Peace on earth will surely grow,
When there's love, that all we know,
If love is freely shared,
Then us there anything to be scared?

Peace on earth will surely grow,
If love like water, purely flow,
Try to give everytime you take,
Peace is ours to make or break.

Peace on earth will surely grow,
Might be tough, might be slow,
But with care, close and near,
There's nothing we should fear

27. MY SUPERHERO

My Superhero

Here in my heart
my daddy will stay.
He nurtured and cared
he held me tight when I was scared.
my best friend, my teacher in life
I saw the tears in my daddy's eyes
when I said I love you
I meant it so deeply
you always carried me to bed
whenever I got sleepy.
You tried to do my hair
and got it tangled every time
but I never cared
playing the guitar, strum at a time
while I danced around you
You never once sighed
I'm your little girl, and I always will be
Even when I forty, I'll still sit on your knee
This day is yours I want to say
I love you dearly!

28. BEST VERSION OF YOURSELF

Best Version of Yourself

You might not be perfect all the time,
To be loved by someone
are you changing your shine?
My external appearance,
Might not define beauty,
But pretty is something
My soul defines.
When you wish to fly high,
then what's there to fear of
These people?
Who don't even know you,
You are scared of those little flaws?
You might not be gold,
that always need to shine,
became that small diamond,
which is so hard to find.
In the race of being perfect,
you are making yourself tired,
leave those roads,
which have already been taken,
Better join yourself
from where you are broken.
Love yourself,

Adore yourself,

and then you become

The Best Version of Yourself!

29. IF YOU CAN SEE

If you can see

If only you can see my eyes now
you will read all the untold words
If only you can see through them
you will understand that for me you are the world

If only you can see the smile on my face
when i receive your email, message or phone call
you will know that you have captured me all

If only you can see what happens to me the moment we meet
If only you can feel how fast my heart beat
you will know that you are the only one who makes me feel
complete

30. WAVES OF LOVE

Waves of Love

With the name of yours,
my eyes do shine
Oh! my love,
As mush as your presence in my life
confuses me right now
I've never been more thankful to you.
The warmth of your arms,
smell, touch and comfort of yours
can never leave my soul alone, no matter
how hard I try.
Waves of complete and utter confusion
keeps on forcing me to ride on,
Oh! my love,
How much do I need
to prevent my heart from falling for you.
I've lost you and
this sense is so hurting,
Yes,
I still love you and I'll till I die,
though I cried even harder than I knew
my body was capable of
made myself sick
with your thoughts

just want to wash away

those memories of yours.

In the midst of all my hatred,

there are waves of reasoning

that flows through me,

it eats at me little by little

wearing down the strength

my hatred lends to me.

Never felt this alone,

This broken,

This angry,

This hurt.

Whenever I remember you

your harsh words cut through me,

still don't know why so stupid am I?

Wanting you back, those abusive words back?

may be it's all because of the waves of

Love I had!

www.ingramcontent.com/pod-product-compliance
Lightning Source LLC
Chambersburg PA
CBHW021545150726
47990CB00006B/2413